Watch It Grow

Painted Lady Butterflies

by Martha E. H. Rustad

Consulting editor: Gail Saunders-Smith, PhD

Consultant: Laura Jesse
Plant and Insect Diagnostic Clinic
Iowa State University, Ames, Iowa

Capstone
press®

Mankato, Minnesota

Pebble Books are published by Capstone Press,
151 Good Counsel Drive, P.O. Box 669, Mankato, Minnesota 56002.
www.capstonepress.com

1 2 3 4 5 6 14 13 12 11 10 09

Library of Congress Cataloging-in-Publication Data
Rustad, Martha E. H. (Martha Elizabeth Hillman), 1975–
    Painted lady butterflies / by Martha E.H. Rustad.
    p. cm. — (Pebble books. Watch it grow)
    Includes bibliographical references and index.
    Summary: "Simple text and photographs present the life cycle of painted lady
butterflies" — Provided by publisher.
    ISBN-13: 978-1-4296-2228-8 (hardcover)   ISBN-10: 1-4296-2228-8 (hardcover)
    ISBN-13: 978-1-4296-3445-8 (softcover)   ISBN-10: 1-4296-3445-6 (softcover)
    1. Painted lady (Insect) — Life cycles — Juvenile literature. I. Title.
QL561.N9R87 2009
595.78'9 — dc22   2008026940

Note to Parents and Teachers

The Watch It Grow set supports national science standards related
to life science. This book describes and illustrates painted lady
butterflies. The images support early readers in understanding
the text. The repetition of words and phrases helps early readers
learn new words. This book also introduces early readers to
subject-specific vocabulary words, which are defined in the
Glossary section. Early readers may need assistance to read some
words and to use the Table of Contents, Glossary, Read More,
Internet Sites, and Index sections of the book.

Table of Contents

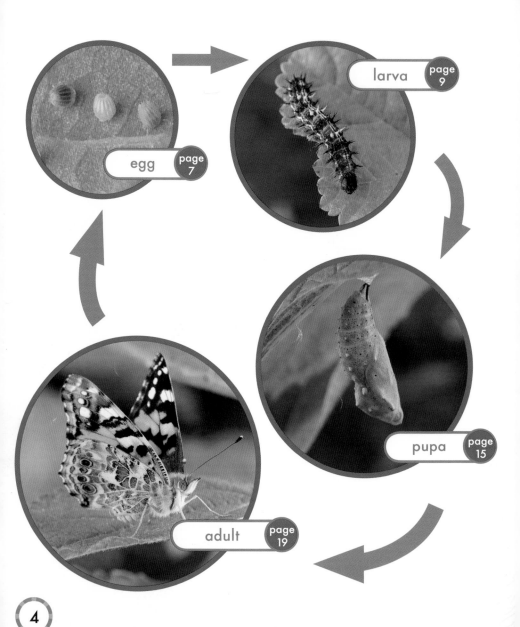

larva page 9

egg page 7

pupa page 15

adult page 19

Metamorphosis

Painted lady butterflies are colorful insects. These butterflies go through metamorphosis as they grow.

eggs

From Egg to Larva

A painted lady butterfly begins life as an egg. A female sticks a tiny egg onto the bottom of a leaf.

caterpillar

After three to five days,
a caterpillar hatches
from the egg.
A caterpillar is
also called a larva.

The caterpillar eats
all the time.
Painted lady caterpillars
eat the leaves of thistles,
sunflowers, and hollyhocks.

The caterpillar sheds its skin, or molts, four times. The caterpillar hangs upside down before its last molt. It is five to 10 days old.

chrysalis

From Pupa to Adult

The caterpillar molts
one last time.
Now it is a pupa.
A hard, green case called
a chrysalis forms around it.

Inside the chrysalis,
the painted lady butterfly
grows wings and legs.

The chrysalis cracks
after five to seven days.
An adult painted lady
butterfly squeezes out.

The butterfly has six legs
and four wings.
It waits for its wings to dry.
Soon it's ready to fly.

Glossary

chrysalis — a hard shell that surrounds a developing butterfly

hatch — to break out of an egg

insect — a small animal with a hard outer shell, six legs, three body sections, and two antennae; most insects have wings.

larva — an insect at the stage between egg and pupa; the plural of larva is larvae.

metamorphosis — the series of changes some animals go through as they develop from eggs to adults

molt — to shed skin or an outer shell so a new covering can be seen; when this process happens once, it is also called a molt.

pupa — an insect at the stage between a larva and an adult; the plural of pupa is pupae.

Read More

Huseby, Victoria. *Butterfly.* Looking at Life Cycles. Mankato, Minn.: Smart Apple Media, 2009.

Rau, Dana Meachen. *The Butterfly in the Sky.* Benchmark Rebus. New York: Marshall Cavendish Benchmark, 2007.

Internet Sites

FactHound offers a safe, fun way to find educator-approved Internet sites related to this book.

Here's what you do:

1. Visit *www.facthound.com*
2. Choose your grade level.
3. Begin your search.

This book's ID number is 9781429622288.

FactHound will fetch the best sites for you!

Index

Word Count: 162
Grade: 1
Early-Intervention Level: 16

Editorial Credits
Erika L. Shores, editor; Alison Thiele, designer; Marcie Spence, photo researcher

Photo Credits
Capstone Press/Karon Dubke, cover (caterpillar and chrysalis), 4 (all), 6 (both), 8, 10, 14, 16, 20
Getty Images Inc./Michael Durham/Minden Pictures, 12, 18
Shutterstock/Christian Musat, cover (adult); Howard Sandler, 1